The power of Protestant religious principle in producing a national spirit of defence, exemplified in a diary of the siege of London-derry. Written by the Rev. George Walker, ...

George Walker

The power of Protestant religious principle in producing a national spirit of defence, exemplified in a diary of the siege of London-derry. Written by the Rev. George Walker, ...
Walker, George, D.D., Governor of Londonderry
ESTCID: T086114
Reproduction from British Library
P.iii misnumbered ii.
London : printed for L. Davis and C. Reymers, 1758.
xii,x,73,[1]p. ; 8°

Eighteenth Century
Collections Online
Print Editions

Gale ECCO Print Editions

Relive history with *Eighteenth Century Collections Online*, now available in print for the independent historian and collector. This series includes the most significant English-language and foreign-language works printed in Great Britain during the eighteenth century, and is organized in seven different subject areas including literature and language; medicine, science, and technology; and religion and philosophy. The collection also includes thousands of important works from the Americas.

The eighteenth century has been called "The Age of Enlightenment." It was a period of rapid advance in print culture and publishing, in world exploration, and in the rapid growth of science and technology – all of which had a profound impact on the political and cultural landscape. At the end of the century the American Revolution, French Revolution and Industrial Revolution, perhaps three of the most significant events in modern history, set in motion developments that eventually dominated world political, economic, and social life.

In a groundbreaking effort, Gale initiated a revolution of its own: digitization of epic proportions to preserve these invaluable works in the largest online archive of its kind. Contributions from major world libraries constitute over 175,000 original printed works. Scanned images of the actual pages, rather than transcriptions, recreate the works ***as they first appeared.***

Now for the first time, these high-quality digital scans of original works are available via print-on-demand, making them readily accessible to libraries, students, independent scholars, and readers of all ages.

For our initial release we have created seven robust collections to form one the world's most comprehensive catalogs of 18th century works.

Initial Gale ECCO Print Editions collections include:

> ### *History and Geography*
> Rich in titles on English life and social history, this collection spans the world as it was known to eighteenth-century historians and explorers. Titles include a wealth of travel accounts and diaries, histories of nations from throughout the world, and maps and charts of a world that was still being discovered. Students of the War of American Independence will find fascinating accounts from the British side of conflict.

Social Science
Delve into what it was like to live during the eighteenth century by reading the first-hand accounts of everyday people, including city dwellers and farmers, businessmen and bankers, artisans and merchants, artists and their patrons, politicians and their constituents. Original texts make the American, French, and Industrial revolutions vividly contemporary.

Medicine, Science and Technology
Medical theory and practice of the 1700s developed rapidly, as is evidenced by the extensive collection, which includes descriptions of diseases, their conditions, and treatments. Books on science and technology, agriculture, military technology, natural philosophy, even cookbooks, are all contained here.

Literature and Language
Western literary study flows out of eighteenth-century works by Alexander Pope, Daniel Defoe, Henry Fielding, Frances Burney, Denis Diderot, Johann Gottfried Herder, Johann Wolfgang von Goethe, and others. Experience the birth of the modern novel, or compare the development of language using dictionaries and grammar discourses.

Religion and Philosophy
The Age of Enlightenment profoundly enriched religious and philosophical understanding and continues to influence present-day thinking. Works collected here include masterpieces by David Hume, Immanuel Kant, and Jean-Jacques Rousseau, as well as religious sermons and moral debates on the issues of the day, such as the slave trade. The Age of Reason saw conflict between Protestantism and Catholicism transformed into one between faith and logic -- a debate that continues in the twenty-first century.

Law and Reference
This collection reveals the history of English common law and Empire law in a vastly changing world of British expansion. Dominating the legal field is the *Commentaries of the Law of England* by Sir William Blackstone, which first appeared in 1765. Reference works such as almanacs and catalogues continue to educate us by revealing the day-to-day workings of society.

Fine Arts
The eighteenth-century fascination with Greek and Roman antiquity followed the systematic excavation of the ruins at Pompeii and Herculaneum in southern Italy; and after 1750 a neoclassical style dominated all artistic fields. The titles here trace developments in mostly English-language works on painting, sculpture, architecture, music, theater, and other disciplines. Instructional works on musical instruments, catalogs of art objects, comic operas, and more are also included.

The BiblioLife Network

This project was made possible in part by the BiblioLife Network (BLN), a project aimed at addressing some of the huge challenges facing book preservationists around the world. The BLN includes libraries, library networks, archives, subject matter experts, online communities and library service providers. We believe every book ever published should be available as a high-quality print reproduction; printed on-demand anywhere in the world. This insures the ongoing accessibility of the content and helps generate sustainable revenue for the libraries and organizations that work to preserve these important materials.

The following book is in the "public domain" and represents an authentic reproduction of the text as printed by the original publisher. While we have attempted to accurately maintain the integrity of the original work, there are sometimes problems with the original work or the micro-film from which the books were digitized. This can result in minor errors in reproduction. Possible imperfections include missing and blurred pages, poor pictures, markings and other reproduction issues beyond our control. Because this work is culturally important, we have made it available as part of our commitment to protecting, preserving, and promoting the world's literature.

GUIDE TO FOLD-OUTS MAPS and OVERSIZED IMAGES

The book you are reading was digitized from microfilm captured over the past thirty to forty years. Years after the creation of the original microfilm, the book was converted to digital files and made available in an online database.

In an online database, page images do not need to conform to the size restrictions found in a printed book. When converting these images back into a printed bound book, the page sizes are standardized in ways that maintain the detail of the original. For large images, such as fold-out maps, the original page image is split into two or more pages

Guidelines used to determine how to split the page image follows:

• Some images are split vertically; large images require vertical and horizontal splits.
• For horizontal splits, the content is split left to right.
• For vertical splits, the content is split from top to bottom.
• For both vertical and horizontal splits, the image is processed from top left to bottom right.

The Power of Protestant religious Principle in producing a national Spirit of Defence,

EXEMPLIFIED IN A

DIARY

OF THE

Siege of *LONDON-DERRY.*

Written by
The Rev. GEORGE WALKER, D.D.
Who commanded the Garrison during the Siege.

Now published, as an *useful Lesson* to the PRESENT TIMES.

To which is prefixed,
A PREFATORY ADDRESS to the Public,
By the EDITOR.

Heu, Pietas! Heu, prisca FIDES!

LONDON:
Printed for L. DAVIS and C. REYMERS,
against *Gray's-Inn, Holborn.* MDCCLVIII.
[Price One Shilling and Sixpence.]

PREFATORY ADDRESS TO THE PUBLIC.

THE Author of the *Estimate of the Manners and Principles of the Times* having explained * at large by what Means and in what Particulars the Popish religious Principle is naturally more permanent than that of Protestantism; and having, perhaps, in the Opinion of some, left the Matter short, in not enlarging on the Efficacy of the Protestant Religion, as a strong Principle of National Valour and Defence; the Editor of the following DIARY was of Opinion, that he could not give a more striking and conclusive Proof of the Power of true Protestant Principle to this great End, than in publishing the following *Memoirs* of the *Siege* of LONDON-DERRY.

Vol. II. p. 127, &c.

HE needs hardly inform the judicious Reader, that they are written with a Simplicity and Modesty, which might have become JULIUS CÆSAR himself: And as to the ACTION *recorded*; the Editor scruples not to give his Opinion, that it is among the *greatest* and most *heroic* that have been delivered down to us in Story.

YET, for many Years past, it hath been almost sunk in Oblivion. Most People, indeed, may have heard, in cold and general Terms, that one Dr. WALKER, a Protestant Clergyman, did defend and preserve LONDON-DERRY in Favour of King WILLIAM the Third, when besieged by *James* the Second, with a numerous Army under his Command. But the particular Circumstances of this astonishing Event, which would have made one of the finest Chapters in the History of a LIVY, are no where to be found, that the Editor knows of, but in the obscure and almost forgotten Tract, which is here again brought to Light.

WHAT must give every Reader the greater Pleasure, is, the undoubted Authenticity

thenticity of the Facts related: As they are recorded by *him* who was the principal Actor during the Siege; who was personally present at all the bold Transactions he relates; who was the Soul and Spirit of the Body of Protestants united in one common Danger; who inspired their Councils, headed their Defence, quelled their Mutinies, animated their Constancy, nay, even commanded (when it was necessary) their Sallies on the Enemy, yet tells his Story with a Modesty so engaging, that it is left (as it were) to the Reader's Sagacity to find out, that Dr. WALKER was more than a simple Citizen *.

* It may, perhaps, gratify the Reader's Curiosity, to know, that this extraordinary Person was born of *English* Parents, in the County of *Tyrone*, was educated in the University of *Glasgow*; and was Rector of *Donaghmore* in *Tyrone*, at the Time of the SIEGE. After the Siege was raised, he went into *England*, where he was graciously received by WILLIAM the Third; was highly caressed by his Court, and by the Citizens of *London*: Was persecuted by the Calumny of wicked Men, who envied him the Glory he had acquired, in the Defence of *Londonderry*. In his Return towards *Ireland*, had the Degree of Doctor in Divinity conferred on him by the University of

But tho' *he*, as *Principal*, claims the first Place in our Admiration, yet every Individual concerned in that glorious Defence, is intitled to the Appellation of the *Friend of his Country.* Most of their Names, indeed, are buried in Oblivion: But *that* is a Matter of the less Consequence; because they acted on a higher Principle than that of human Glory, and have, independent of Mankind, obtained the great Reward they fought for.

As a mere Curiosity, the Journal of this gallant Defence might deserve the Notice of the Public: But the Editor views it in a higher Light, and would recommend it as a useful Lesson to his Countrymen, in the following Variety of Respects.

1. It may stand as a concurrent Proof of what the Author of the *Estimate* asserted, " That at the Period when this

---

Oxford. Thence he went into *Ireland*, where, having a Command given him in the *English* Army, he was killed on the first Onset, at the Battle of the Boyne.   See Wood's *Athenæ Oxon.*

" Event

"Event happened, the Protestant Princi-
"ple took the Lead, even of the Spirit of
"civil Libery; and effected the most glo-
"rious Revolution that History hath yet
"recorded: A Revolution, which might
"justly be styled *religious* rather than *po-*
"*litical**."

2. The Facts here recorded, afford a striking Instance of another of his Observ-tions: "That Popish Superstition is a
"more active Principle, with Regard to
"Conquest, than rational Protestantism.
"That the first piques itself on destroying
"and extirpating the Enemies of God;
"while the latter, regarding none as the
"Enemies of God on Account of Error,
"aims only at rational Defence†."

3. It may stand as a concurrent Proof of another of his Assertions; That "while
"Protestantism retains its proper *Influence*
"in the Minds of Men, it may be a

---

* *Estimate*, Vol. II. p. 139,—140.
† *Ibid.* p. 128.

"Match

"Match for Popish Superstition: That what it wants in *Fury*, it makes up in *Steadiness**.

4. It may tend to convince every Rank of Men in this Kingdom, during the present neglected State of Religion, what a powerful Principle of Action and Defence is now, by some Means or other, lost among them. Let every Man impartially examine himself, Whether, under the like Circumstances, he would be animated by a Regard to true Religion and Christianity, to act as bold and disinterested a Part, as the Gentlemen, the Clergy, and common People, performed, in this severe Trial of their Courage and Constancy. Let every Man, after examining his own Breast, look round among his Neighbours and Countrymen, and calmly consider, if there be one Symptom left, that can induce him to believe, that the same Spirit of Fortitude now exists among us. If not; then let every Man impartially examine the Causes, that may

---

* *Estimate*, Vol. II. p. 128.

have concurred in the Production of a Change of Manners and Principles, so much to be lamented, because so fatal to the Stability of the Common-Weal. Let him consider how far the Introduction of exorbitant *Wealth*, the general Attention to *Gain*, to *Luxury*, and *Pleasure*, together with the *Abuse* of civil Liberty, have tended to relax those Principles of Religion, (and therefore of *Government*) which worked such Wonders but Seventy Years ago: Let him consider this, I say; let him then weigh those Representations that have been lately made of the State of this Kingdom, with Regard to *Manners* and *Principles*, and determine concerning their *Truth* or *Falshood*.

5. IT may be regarded as a Proof, how great public Service a rational, active, and zealous Clergy may do to the Common-wealth, when they are held in due Esteem by their Country: And may therefore discover the Imprudence of any Party, or any Age, in loading them

them with general Characters of undeserved Contempt.

6. It may furnish us with a Proof, that both Leaders and Troops may be found among the Body of a People, aided by a very moderate Share of external Discipline, yet sufficient for the Defence of their Country, provided only they be *inwardly disciplined* by proper *Principles* and *Manners*. It may convince us, that an Army or a Kingdom seemingly strong in the Arts and Nerves of War, may be in Truth a dead and inactive Mass, void of all Energy and Power: while another Army or Kingdom, in all Appearance destitute of the Resources of Wealth, Numbers, and external Discipline, shall by the mere internal Vigour of Religion and Virtue, combat and overwhelm its most formidable Enemies.

7. The Gentlemen of the Army may see, how efficacious that Principle of Religion is, which they have not only blindly neglected to cultivate, both in themselves and among their Troops, but have even
too

too generally (tho' not without Exceptions which deserve the highest Praise) attempted to discourage and banish from the Heart of every Soldier; regarding it as a Principle inconsistent with Courage, and too frequently substituting *Brandy* and *Profligacy* in its Stead. They will here see the essential Difference between the temporary Flashes of that artificial Courage, which these adventitious Aids can inspire, and that steady and determined Spirit of Defence, which is the Result of upright Principle.

They may here read, and blush for the Conduct of some of their own Profession, who dissuaded the brave Inhabitants from attempting a Defence; and basely quitted the City in an ignominious Disguise, even before it was attacked, or invested. They may see, that neither Courage nor military Honour are confined to any Profession or Rank of Men: They have here a noble Example of Fortitude in those who followed not the Trade of War, sufficient, surely, to animate those who do, to a brave and unconquerable Defence, in those Forts,

Garrisons, Cities, or Commands, which may be given to their Charge by their King and their Country: An Example, which if attended to and followed, will of course endear them to their Fellow-Citizens, and transmit their Names with Honour to Posterity.

TO

Their Sacred MAJESTIES,

William and Mary,

KING and QUEEN

OF

*ENGLAND, SCOTLAND,
FRANCE* and *IRELAND.*

May it pleafe your Majefties,

NEXT to the Pleafure of doing well, there is no greater Satisfaction than where the Performance meets with a favourable Reception from thofe for whofe Sake it is defigned. I thank God, I have this double Comfort in the Teftimony of a good Confcience,

and

and your Majesties Gracious Acceptance of the poor Services God enabled me to do for your Majesties Interest, and the Safety of those Protestants, whom the Fury of the *Papists* drove into *London-derry*.

Nor am I more pleased with Your Majesties Royal Bounty to me, much above not only my Merit, but Expectation, than with Your Majesties Tenderness for my poor Fellow-Sufferers and Partners in that Action, whom I doubt not but Your Majesties will find as brave in the Field, and in taking other Towns, as in defending that, which neither the Number, nor Rage of their Enemies without, nor those more cruel ones within, of Famine and Sickness, could ever make them think of Surrendering. " The Part I acted in " this Service might more properly have " been done by other Hands, but that " Necessity which threw it upon me,
" will

"will, I hope, juftify me before God
"and the World, from the Irregularity
"of interefting myfelf in fuch an Affair,
"for which I was neither by Education
"or Function qualified; efpecially, fince
"the Neceffity which called me to it,
"was no fooner over, than I refigned
"more chearfully than ever I undertook
"the Employment, that I might ap-
"ply myfelf to the Plough to which I
"had fet my Hand." I am not at all
angry with the Reflections that fome
make, as they think, to my Difparage-
ment; becaufe all they fay of this Kind,
gives God the greater Honour, in whofe
Almighty Hand no Inftrument is weak,
in whofe Prefence no Flefh muft glory.
"But as the whole Conduct of this
"Matter muft be afcribed to Providence
"alone, as it ought, this fhould then
"give them Occafion to confider that
"God has efpoufed your Majefties Caufe,

"and

"and fights your Battles, and for the
"Proteſtant Religion; and by making
"Uſe of a poor Miniſter, the unworthi-
"eſt of the whole Communion of which
"he is a Member, would intimate to
"the World, by what Hand he will
"defend and maintain both Your Ma-
"jeſties Intereſt, and the Religion you
"have delivered from thoſe that were
"ready to ſwallow both up."

THAT which I here preſume to lay at Your Majeſties Feet, is, indeed, very unfit for Your Royal View; but that ſince Importunity would have it publick, I thought it Sacrilege to entitle any other to the Copy, than thoſe to whom the Original was devoted. The Picture cannot be commended for the Workmanſhip, but it may poſſibly be the more acceptable, for that becauſe more reſembling the Life from which it is drawn:

drawn: There is little Skill, or Art, in either, but there are Ornaments much more valuable in both, natural Simplicity, Sincerity, and a plain Truth, in which Character I humbly beg Your Majesties will always consider, and accept the Endeavours of

Your Majesties most obliged,

Most faithful, and most obedient

Subject and Servant,

GEORGE WALKER.

A DESCRIPTION OF THE CITY OF LONDON-DERRY.

THE Form of the Town comes somewhat near an *Oblong-Square*, or a long Square; and it's Situation Lengthwise is *N. W.* and *S. E.* or on a Diagonal drawn from the Church through the Market-house to the Magazine, is near upon a *North* and *South* Line.

THE Length of the Town through the Middle from *Ship-key Gate* to *Bishopsgate*, is about 300 Paces, or 1500 Foot. The Wall on the *West* Side of the Town 320 Paces; the Wall on the *East* about 380.

THE Breadth at *N. W.* End 140; at the *S. E.* End 120; from *Butchers-gate* to Ferry-

Ferry-gate, where the Town is broadeſt, 180 Paces.

The Wall is generally ſeven or eight Foot thick; but the Outſide Wall of Stone, or Battlements above the *Terra-plene*, is not more than two Foot in Thickneſs.

The four Corners have each of them a Baſtion; on the long Side the *Weſtward* are two other Baſtions; and on the Side to the *Eaſtward*, one Baſtion, one Demi-Baſtion, and two other Works which are commonly called Platforms.

There are four Gates; *Biſhops-gate* at the *S. E.* End: *Ship-key Gate* at the End oppoſite to it: *Butchers-gate* at the *N. E.* Side, and *Ferry-key-gate* over againſt it.

In the Middle of the Town is a *Square*, called the *Diamond*; where the *Market-houſe*

house stands (during the Siege, turned into a *Guard-house*).

NEAR the *S W.* End of the Town stands the Church, on the Top whereof, being a flat Roof, were placed two of our Guns, which were of great Use in annoying the Enemy. In the *S. E.* Angle of the Town, was the principal Magazine. Within the Town also were several Wells; and before *Bishops-gate* was a *Ravelin* built by Colonel *Lundy*, and the Ground on forwards to the *Wind-mill-hill*, was taken in by the Besieged to the Distance of 260 Paces from the Town, and about the same Distance a-cross from the River; and for Fear this Ground should be taken from the Besieged by the Enemy, another Line was industriously drawn from the *S. W.* Quarter of the Town to the River, to secure their Retreat.

The Number of Guns placed on the Bastions and Line, was eight *Sakers* and twelve *Demi-culverins*.

The whole Town stands upon an easy Ascent, and exposed most of the Houses to the Enemy's Guns.

A DIARY

OF THE

SIEGE of *LONDON-DERRY*.

BEING prevailed on to give an Account of the Siege of *London-Derry*, it is convenient, by Way of Preliminary, to take Notice how that Town came to be out of the Hands of the *Irish*, when all Places of the Kingdom, of any Strength or Consideration, were possessed by them. It pleased God so to infatuate the Councils of my Lord *Tyrconnel*, that when the 3000 Men were sent to *England* to assist his Master against the Invasion of the Prince of *Orange*, he took particular Care to send away the whole Regiment quartered in and about this City. He soon saw his Error, and endeavoured to repair it, by commanding my

Lord *Antrim* to quarter there with his Regiment, consisting of a numerous Swarm of *Irish* and *Highlanders*. Upon the 6th of *December*, they were on their March in and about *New-Town*, a Market Town belonging to Col. *George Philips*, twelve Miles distant from *Derry*. Col. *Philips* having Notice of this, and joining with it the Apprehensions they were under, of a general Insurrection of the *Irish* intended on the 9th of *December*; and considering that *Derry*, as well as other Places, is to be presently possessed by the *Irish*; and having several Informations brought him, and some taken before him that gave some credit to the Fear and Jealousies they were under, and encreased his Suspicion of some damnable Design against the *British* of those Parts, he immediately dispatches a Letter to Alderman *Norman*, giving an Account of these Matters, and his Opinion of them, and importuning him to consult with the sober People of the Town, and to set out the Danger of admitting such Guests among them. The next Day he sent an Express, advising him to cause the Gates of the City to be shut, and assured them he would be with them with his

Friends

Friends the Day following, and would stand by them and serve them to the Hazard of his Life and Fortune. Alderman *Norman* and the rest of the graver Citizens were under great Disorder and Consternation, and knew not what to resolve upon. One of the Companies was already in View of the Town, and two of the Officers within it; but the younger Sort, who are seldom so dilatory in their Resolutions, got together, run in all Haste to the Main-Guard, snatch'd up the Keys, and immediately shut up all the four Gates, and the Magazine. On the 9th Day, Col. *Philips* comes into *London-derry*. He had been Governour of that Town, as also of the Fort of *Culmore* in King *Charles's* Time, and therefore the Inhabitants desire him to resume the Government, and immediately delivered him the Keys of the Gates and the Magazine. He being well acquainted with Proceedings in *England*, with the Advice of the gravest Sort, dispatches Mr. *David Kerns* as their Agent thither, to represent their Condition and Resolutions, and to procure some speedy Relief.

NEWS

News being carried to *Dublin* of this Revolt, as they call'd it, the Lord *Mont-joy*, with his Lieutenant-Colonel *Lundy* and six Companies, are sent down to reduce the Place. The Governour had already form'd eight Companies of good effectual Men in the City, and armed them out of the Stores; and with some Management quieted all Factions and Tumults, and reduced all Things to good Order; so that all were unanimously resolved to stand it out till they received a Return to their Address sent into *England*. My Lord *Montjoy* appears before the Town, his Interest among us, and the Consideration of our own Circumstances, that there was no Appearance of any sudden Relief from *England*, no Provisions in the Town, and (which was worst of all) but two Barrels of Powder in the Magazine, which my Lord *Montjoy* must needs understand, being Master of the Ordnance; it was thought most adviseable to listen to a Treaty. So the Governour, with the Consent of the City-council, agreed upon certain Capitulations; that only two Companies should enter the Town, and they to be all Protestants; and that the Town-companies

companies should be allowed to keep their Arms, and to do duty with the others, and that no Stranger is to be admitted into the City, without License from the Governor and Sheriffs. Having obtained Conditions of so easy a Nature, and of so probable Advantage to the Town, they received my Lord *Montjoy*, who made Lieutenant-Colonel *Lundy*, Governor of the Town.

The Gentlemen of the other Parts of the north of *Ireland*, being well acquainted with the Proceedings at *Dublin*; that particularly Commissions were given out to raise many Thousands of *Irish*, all over the Kingdom, and all to be maintained at the Expence of their Officers (who were not able to support themselves) for the Space of three Months. They were with good Reason apprehensive, this was not intended for their Satisfaction or Advantage; and therefore they generally resolved to put themselves in the best Posture they could to defend themselves against any Inconveniencies such Methods might bring upon them. They had several Consultations with their Neighbours, and some great Men were

not

not wanting in their Advice and Encouragement. One left some Instructions with Mr. *George Walker*, Rector of *Donaghmore*, in the County of *Tyrone*, recommending the Necessity of securing *Dungannon* by a Garrison of their own, and of victualling that Town. " In order to
" which Mr. *Walker* saw it not only ex-
" cusable, but necessary to concern him-
" self, and raise Men, out of which he
" formed a Regiment, and to apply what
" Interest he could make towards the
" Preservation of that Town." *Gordon O'Neale*, observing those Preparations, sends his Priest to enquire into the Meaning of them, which was readily interpreted to him: *So many* Irish *were armed in the Country, they thought fit to put themselves in a Posture of Defence against the Danger they saw themselves exposed to.* The Men complain of Want of Powder, but by the Contrivance of their Officer, a Bag of *Mustard-seed* was laid upon the Carriages, which, by it's Resemblance, easily obtained the Credit of a Bag of Powder, and immediately gave Motion to the Soldiers.

In order to settle a Correspondence with *London-derry*, Mr. *Walker* rides to that Town, and consults Col. *Lundy* The Opinion they had of his Experience in War, and Zeal for the Cause they were to maintain, gave all People great Expectation from his Conduct; he approves and encourages the Design, sends two Files of his disciplined Men to *Dungannon*, and afterwards two Troops of Dragoons.

March 14. Orders are sent to Colonel *Steward* (who was very considerable among us) from Col. *Lundy*, that the Garrison at *Dungannon* should break up; some, considering the advantageous Situation of the Place, and the great Quantity of Provisions already laid in, and the Consequence at leaving both to give Strength to their Enemies, shewed some Unwillingness to comply with Commands so different from the Measures they had hitherto pursued, but at last agreed to march to *Colrain* or *Derry*, according to Col. *Lundy's* Orders.

March 17. We marched as far as *Strabane*, and there met our Order from Col. *Lundy* to return to *Omagh*, and the *Rash*.

Five

Five Companies of the above Regiment are quartered at *Rash*, under Command of Mr. *Walker*, and five at *Omagh*, commanded by Lieutenant-Colonel *Mervin*: A Fortnight after, we received a Patent to march to *St. Johnstown*, five Miles from *Derry*.

March 20. CAPT. *James Hamilton* arrived from *England* with Ammunition and Arms, 480 Barrels of Powder, and Arms for 2000 Men, and a Commission from the King and Queen for Col. *Lundy* to be Governor of the City, together with Instructions to swear all Officers military and civil, and Assurance of speedy Supplies from *England*. The King and Queen are publickly proclaimed with great Joy and Solemnity. About this Time the *Irish* made a Descent into *Ulster*, and drove great Numbers of poor *Protestants* before them, who took Shelter in *Colrain* and *London-derry*.

March 23. COL. *Philips* is sent to *England* with an Address to the King, and to follicit a speedy Supply.

COL.

Col. *Lundy* goes to *Colrain* to give his Advice and Assistance to that Place. The rest of this Month, and the Beginning of the next, is spent in Preparations against the Enemy; they had possessed themselves of *Colrain*, and drove all before them till they came to *Clody-bridge*, of which you have already had a short Account.

April 13. Mr. *Walker* receiving Intelligence that the Enemy was drawing towards *Derry*, he rides in all Haste thither, and gives Col *Lundy* an Account of it, but the Colonel believed it only a false Alarm. Mr. *Walker* returns from him to *Lyfford*, where he joined Col. *R Crofton*: The Enemy come to *Clody-ford*; all Night long the Enemy and we fired at one another, and in the Morning Mr. *Walker* took his Post at the Long Causey, as commanded by Col. *Lundy*, leaving Col. *Crofton* to maintain the Post against the Enemy, which he performed with good Resolution.

The Soldiers having spent all their Ammunition, are forced to give Way. Major *Stroud* rallies the Horse, in order to bring off the Foot: The Regiment at the Long Causey

Causey staid too long, expecting Order[s] but got off under the Shelter of som[e] Horse, and followed the Army, whic[h] was 10,000 strong, and making good the Retreat to *Derry*; Col. *Lundy* and sever[al] of Quality being then at the Head of the[m] Mr. *Walker* found the Gates shut again[st] him and his Regiment: They stay a [?] Night without the Gates: Next Day wit[h] much Difficulty, and some Violence upo[n] the Centry, they got in: Mr. *Walk[er]* waited on Col. *Lundy*, and pressed th[e] taking the Field; but he not being satisfie[d] with the Behaviour of his Army the Da[y] before, gave Advice of a different Natur[e]
" which did not agree with Mr *Walker*[s]
" Sentiments, who thought himself oblige[d]
" to stand by his Men that he had brough[t]
" from their own Homes, and not to ex[-]
" pose them again to the Enemy."

April 15. Col. *Cunningham* and Co[l.] *Richards* come into the Lough from *Eng[-]land*, with two Regiments, and other Ne[-]cessaries, for Supply of *Derry*.

There were several remarkable Passa[-]ges might be here inserted, relating to thos[e] tha[t] that came from *Drumore* and *Colrain*; but as I would not reproach any, so I cannot do right to all; and whatever Misfortune the Difficulty of those Places brought upon them, the Behaviour of such of them as staid in the Garrison of *Derry*, sets them above Apologies for any Miscarriage; for certainly there could not be better Men in the World; and many of those that left us have been exposed to Censure; but I hope the World will be so just, not to give Characters from Things done in such a Confusion.

April 17. Upon the News of King *James's* Army being on their March towards *London-derry*, " Colonel *Lundy*, " our Governor, thought fit to call a Coun- " cil; and ordered that Col. *Cuningham*, and " Col. *Richards*, who were sent from " *England* to our Assistance, should be " Members of it." Accordingly they met, and with other Gentlemen equally unacquainted with the Condition of the Town, or the Inclination and Resolution of the People, they make this following Order:

" *UPON*

"UPON Enquiry it appears, Th[at] there is not Provision in the Garrison [of] London-derry, for the present Garris[on] and the two Regiments on board, for abo[ut] a Week, or ten Days at most: And it a[p]pearing that the Place is not tenable again[st] a well-appointed Army; Therefore it [is] concluded upon, and resolved, That it [is] not convenient for his Majesty's Servic[e,] but the contrary, to land the two Reg[i]ments under Col. Cunningham and C[ol.] Richards, their Command now on boar[d] in the River of Lough-foyle.——Th[at] considering the present Circumstances [of] Affairs, and the Likelihood the Enemy w[ill] soon possess themselves of this Place, it [is] thought most convenient, that the princip[al] Officers shall privately withdraw them[selves, as well for their own Preservatio[n] as in Hopes that the Inhabitants, by [a] timely Capitulation, may make Terms t[he] better with the Enemy; and that this [we] judge most convenient for his Majest[y's] Service, as the present State of Affai[rs] now is."

AFTER this Resolution, an Instrumen[t] was prepared to be subscribed by the Ge[n]tleme[n] tlemen of the Council, and to be sent to King *James*, who was advanced in Person with his Army as far as *St. Johnstown*; it was recommended with this Encouragement; *There was no doubt, but upon surrender of the Town, King* James *would grant a general Pardon, and order Restitution of all that had been plundered from them.* Some Gentlemen were influenced by these Considerations to subscribe, others did not only refuse, but began to conceive some Jealousies of their Governor, and some, tho' they did but guess at their Proceedings, expressed themselves after a ruder Manner, threatening to hang both the Governor and his Council. Capt. *White* is sent out to the King, to receive Proposals from him; and it was at the same Time agreed with Lieutenant-General *Hamilton*, that he should not march the Army within four Miles of the Town.

NOTWITHSTANDING which, King *James* having some Confidence given him, that the Town, upon his Majesty's Approach, would undoubtedly surrender to him, and that the very Sight of so formidable an Army would fright them into a Com-

Compliance: Upon the 18th of *April* advances, with his Army, before our Walls, with flying Colours; his Majesty thinking it Discretion to use the Shelter of a Party of Horse on south end of *Derry-hill*, the more safely to observe what Salutation his Forces had from the Garrison.

Orders were given, that none should dare to fire till the King's Demands were first known, by another Messenger to be sent to his Majesty for that Purpose; but our Men on the Walls, wondering to see Lieut. Gen. *Hamilton* (contrary to his Engagement, not to come within four Miles of the Town) approaching our Walls in such Order, they imagining they were by some Means or other betrayed, thought it reasonable to consider their own Safety, and to keep the Enemy at distance, by firing their Guns upon them, which they accordingly did.

The Enemy that were great Strangers to this Sort of Exercise, upon this could not be kept in any Order by their Officers; but some took to their heels, others with less Labour could hide themselves, and a great

great many were killed King *James* did shew himself in some Disorder, and much surprised to find the Behaviour of his Army, as well as of the besieged, so different from the Character he had received of both. Some were apprehensive of the King's Displeasure upon such a Disappointment, and sent Arch-deacon *Hamilton*, and Mr. *Nevil*, to beg his Majesty's Pardon for having drawn his Majesty into so dangerous and unsuccessful an Undertaking, and to signify to him the Difficulty of commanding or persuading so tumultuous and untractable a Rabble, to any Moderation or Compliance; but if his Majesty drew off his Army, till those Gentlemen returned, and brought Assurance of his Majesty's Presence with it (of which some Question was yet made) they doubted not but they could bring them to a better Understanding.

This Evening King *James* retired with his Army to St. *John's-town*. In the mean time Mr. *Muckcridge* the Town-clerk sees it absolutely necessary to give some Intimation of Proceedings at the Council of War, " which (though every Man's Con-
" cern)

" cern) Care was taken not to make too
" publick, *viz.* That Col. *Cuningham*,
" his Ships, Men, and Provision should
" return to *England*, and all Gentlemen
" and others in Arms should quit the Gar-
" rison, and go along with him this Dif-
" covery occasioned great Uneasiness and
" Disorder in the Town," which had like
to have had very ill Effects upon the Governor and some of his Council, it did also add much to the Rage and Violence
of the Garrison, when they heard some
Wrong had been done my Lord *Kingston*
and his Party, by the indirect Measures
of some within our Walls, their Concern
for him being as great as their Expectations
from him.

" THE Governor and his Council
" finding themselves of little Interest in
" the Town, and that they could not be
" further serviceable, *&c.* thought fit to
" retire, and not to press the Matter fur-
" ther. Some of the Gentlemen left us
" in all this Confusion, and made their
" Escape to the Ships at *Kilmore*, though
" not without some Hazard," for the
Soldiers

Soldiers were under great Discontent, to find themselves deserted by those that engaged them in the Difficulties they were then under, and were not easily kept from expressing it with Violence upon some Persons; but it was the Care of others to keep them in temper, and from those Outrages, as well as to support them against such Discouragements.

Sir *Arthur Royden* protested against the Proceedings of the Council, and would not have left the Town, but that he was dangerously sick, and was forced from us by the Advice of his Physician, and his Friends.

" Governor *Lundy* could not so easily
" make his Escape, being conceived more
" obnoxious than any of the rest, but found
" it convenient to keep his Chamber; a
" Council being appointed, Mr *Walker*
" and Major *Baker* meeting him there, desired him to continue his Government;
" and that he might be assured of all the
" assistance they could give him; but he
" positively refused to concern himself any
" further

" further. The Commission he bore, as
" as well as their Respect for his Person,
" made it a Duty in them to contribute
" all they could to his Safety, and there-
" fore finding him desirous to escape the
" Danger of such a Tumult, they suffered
" him to disguise himself, and in a Sally,
" for the Relief of *Culmore*, to pass in a
" Boat with a Load of Match on his
" Back, from whence he got to the Ship-
" ping."

April 19. THE Garrison seeing they were deserted, and left without a Governor, and having resolved to maintain the Town, and to defend it against the Enemy, they considered of some Person they could have Confidence in, to direct them in the Management of this Affair, " and
" unanimously resolved to chuse Mr. *Wal-*
" *ker* and Major *Baker*, to be their Go-
" vernors during the Siege;" but these Gentlemen, considering the Importance as well as the Uncertainty of such an Office, acquainted, by Letter, Col. *Cunning-ham* (whose Business they thought it was to take Care of them) with this Matter,

and desired him to undertake the Charge; but he being obliged, by his Instructions, to obey the Orders of Col. *Lundy*, thought fit to take other Measures. They then accepted the Government of the Garrison. These Gentlemen chose eight Colonels, and regimented the Men in this Order:

Col. *Walker*	15 Companies.
Col. *Baker*	25 Companies.
Col. *Crofton*	12 Companies.
Col. *Michelturn*	17 Companies, formerly Col. *Skivington's* Regiment.
Col. *Lance*	13 Companies.
Col. *Mountro*	13 Companies, formerly Col *Whitney's*.
Col. *Hamilton*	14 Companies.
Col. *Murrey*	8 Companies.

In all 117 Companies, each Company consisting of 60 Men. In all 7020 Men, 341 Officers.

This was our Complement, after having formed ourselves as above-mentioned; but the Number of Men, Women and Children

Children in the Town was about 30,000
Upon a Declaration of the Enemy to receive and protect all that would desert u[s]
and return to their Dwellings, 10,000 le[ft]
us; after that many more grew weary [of]
us, and 7000 died of Diseases.

THE same Day our Governors view th[e]
Stores, and give other necessary Orders an[d]
Directions: In the mean Time they observ[e]
the Motion of the Enemy, and that thei[r]
Guns were so placed, that they could no[t]
draw out to their usual Place of exercising[;]
therefore they divide the Out-line int[o]
eight Parts: Each Regiment had its ow[n]
Ground, and each Company knew their ow[n]
Bastion. The Drummers were all enjoyn-
ed to quarter in one House, so that on th[e]
least Notice they repaired to the respectiv[e]
Post of the Company they belonged to[;]
and upon all Alarms, without any Parad-
ing, all Officers and private Men came int[o]
their own Ground and Places, without th[e]
least Disorder or Confusion.

"THERE were eighteen Clergymen i[n]
"the Town of the Communion of the
"Church

"Church, who, in their Turns, when
"they were not in Action, had Prayers
"and Sermon every Day; the seven non-
"conforming Ministers were equally care-
"ful of their People, and kept them
"very obedient and quiet," much different from the Behaviour of their Brother
Mr. *Osborn*, who was a Spy upon the
whole North, employed by my Lord *Tyrconnel*, and Mr. *Hewson*, who was very
troublesome, and would admit none to
fight for the *Protestant Religion* till they
had first taken the Covenant.

"AFTER enjoyning all Parties to forget
"their Distinctions, and to join as one
"Man, in Defence of the Interest of
"King *William* and Queen *Mary*, and
"the *Protestant Religion*, against the Ene-
"mies of both; we betake ourselves, in
"the first Place, by Order, to our several
"Devotions, and recommend ourselves,
"and the Cause we undertook, to the
"Protection and Care of the Almighty;
"for we might then truly say, with the
"Church in the *Liturgy*, *There is none
"other that fighteth for us, but only thou,
"O

"*O God.*" It did beget some Disorder amongst us, and Confusion, when we looked about us and saw what we were doing; our Enemies all about us, and our Friends running away from us; a Garrison we had composed of a Number of poor People, frightened from their own Homes; and seemed more fit to hide themselves, than to face an Enemy; when we considered we had no Persons of any Experience in War among us, and those very Persons that were sent to assist us, had so little Confidence in the Place, that they no sooner saw it but they thought fit to leave it: That we had but few Horse to sally out with, and no Forage, no Engineers to instruct us in our Works, no Fire-Works, not as much as a Hand-granado to annoy the Enemy; not a Gun well mounted in the whole Town; that we had so many Mouths to feed, and not above ten Days Provision for them, in the Opinion of our former Governors; that every Day several left us, and gave constant Intelligence to the Enemy, that they had so many Opportunities to divide us, and so often endeavoured it, and to betray the Governors; that they were so numerous, so powerful

and

and well appointed an Army, that in all human Probability we could not think ourſelves in leſs Danger, than the *Iſraelites* at the *Red Sea*.

"WHEN we conſidered all this, it was
"obvious enough what a dangerous Un-
"dertaking we had ventured upon; but
"the Reſolution and Courage of our Peo-
"ple, and the Neceſſity we were under,
"and the great Confidence and Depend-
"ance among us on God Almighty, that
"he would take Care of us and preſerve
"us, made us overlook all thoſe Difficul-
"ties." And God was pleaſed to make us the happy Inſtruments of preſerving this Place, and to him we give the Glory, and no one need go about to undervalue or leſſen thoſe he was pleaſed to chuſe for ſo great a Work. We do allow ourſelves to be as unfit for it as they can make us, and that God has only glorified himſelf in working ſo great a Wonder, *with his own Right Hand, and his holy Arm getting himſelf the Victory.*

April 20. A Part of the Enemy marched towards *Peny-burn-hill*, a Place a Mile distant from the Town *N. by E.* on the Side of the River; there they pitched their Tents, and by that Means hindered all Passage to, and Correspondence with, *Culmore*.

We sent Mr. *Bennet* out of the Garrison, with Orders to go to *England*, and to give Account of our Resolutions to defend the Town against the Enemy. Our Men were ordered to fire after him, that the Enemy might think he had deserted us.

This Day my Lord *Strabane* came up to our Walls, making us many Proposals, and offering *his King's* Pardon, Protection and Favour, if we would surrender the Town; but these fine Words had no Place with the Garrison. At that very Time of his capitulating with us, we observed the Enemy using that Opportunity to draw their Cannon to a convenient Stand; we therefore desired his Lordship to withdraw, otherwise we would make bold to fire at his

his Lordſhip. His Lordſhip continued in his Compliments, till we plainly told him we would never deliver the Town to any but King *William* and Queen *Mary*, or their Order. My Lord having ended all his Inſinuations, found himſelf at laſt obliged to retire.

Several Trumpets were likewiſe ſent, but with as little Succeſs.

April 21. The Enemy placed a *Demiculverin* 180 Perches diſtant from the Town, *E by N.* on the other Side the Water: They play'd at the Houſes in the Town, but did little or no Miſchief, only to the Market-houſe.

This Day our Men ſallied out, as many as pleaſed, and what Officers were at Leiſure, not in any commendable Order, yet they killed above 200 of the Enemy's Soldiers, beſides *Mamow*, the *French* General, and ſeveral other Officers. A Party of Horſe came with great Fury upon the Salliers, and forced their Retreat, which they made good with the Loſs of four

pri-

private Men, and one Lieut. *McPhedris*, whom our Men brought off; and having Leisure and more Concern *then* upon us for the Loss, than afterwards on such Occasions, we buried them with some Ceremony. We had at this Time fifty Horse, commanded by Col. *Murry*, upon whom they pressed so hard at first, that some of his Horse were beaten to the very Gates; " so that Mr. *Walker* found it necessary to " mount one of the Horses and make them " rally, and to relieve Col. *Murry*, whom " he saw surrounded with the Enemy, " and with great Courage laying about " him." In this Action we took three Pair of Colours.

April 23. The Besiegers planted four *Demi-culverins* in the lower End of Mr. *Strong's* Orchard, near eighty Perches distant from the Town, opposite to *Ship-key-street*. These playing incessantly, hurt several People in the Houses, battered the Walls and Garrets, so that none could lodge safely above Stairs. The Besieged make due Returns to their firing from the Bastions, killed Lieut. *Fitz-Patrick*, Lieutenant-Colonel *O'Neale*, two Serjeants, and

several

several Soldiers; and besides these, two *Friars* in their Habits, to the great Grief of the Enemy, that the Blood of those holy Men should be spilt by such an Heretical Rabble, as they called the Besieged.

April 25 THEY place their Mortar-pieces in the said Orchard, and from thence play a few small Bombs, which did little Hurt to the Town, all of them lighting in the Streets, except one, which killed an old Woman in a Garret, from the same Place they threw afterwards many larger Bombs, the first of which fell into a House while several Officers were at Dinner; it fell upon the Bed of the Room they were in, but did not touch any of them, forced into a lower Room, and killed the Landlord; and broke down one Side of the House, and made a large Passage for the Guests to come out, instead of the Door, it had choaked up.

April 28. THE Besieged made another Sally, and killed several of the Enemy at *Penyburn-hill*; but were forced to retreat, being pressed by the Enemy's Horse, who

charged

charged on all Sides. In this Action we lost only two Men; had eight or ten wounded, which in few Days recovered, and were fit for Service.

This Day, by a Shot from one of our Bastions, the Enemy's Gunner was killed, and one of his Guns broken.

May 5. This Night the Besiegers draw a Trench cross the *Windmill-hill,* from the Bog to the River, and there begin a Battery; from that they endeavoured to annoy our Walls, but they were too strong for the Guns they used, " and our Men " were not afraid to advise them to save " all that Labour and Expence; that " they always kept the Gates open, and " they might use that Passage if they " pleased, which was wider than any " Breach they could make in the " Walls."

May 6. The Besieged fearing that Battery might incommode that Part of the Town nearest to it, consult how to put a Stop to their further Proceeding in that Work.

Work. Mr. *Walker* draws a Detachment out of each Company, of ten Men, and after putting them into the best Order their Impatience could allow, he sallies out at the Head of them (with all imaginable Silence) at *Ferry-key-gate*, at four o'Clock in the Morning. One Part of them beat the Enemy's Dragoons from the Hedges, while the other possesses their Trenches. The Dispute was soon over, and the Enemy, though a very considerable Detachment, are so pressed by the Forwardness of our Men, and discouraged at the Sight of so many lying in their Blood, that they fled away, and left us the Ground we contended for, and some Booty, besides the Plunder of the Dead.

The Salliers in this Action killed two Hundred of their Men, most of whom were shot through the Breast or Head; five Hundred were wounded, three Hundred of them within few Days died of their Wounds, as we were informed by Messengers, and the Prisoners we took afterwards. Our Side lost three Men, and

and had only twenty wounded. At [that]
Time we took five Pair of Colours.

We sent a Drummer to desire [the]
Enemy to send an Officer with fourt[een]
Men to bury their Dead, which t[hey]
did perform very negligently, scarce [co]-
vering their Bodies with Earth.

After this Performance, the Enem[y's]
Want of Courage, and our Want of H[orses]
occasioned, that some Weeks produ[ced]
but little of Action, except Skirmish[es.]
Captain *Noble* heads the Men in seve[ral]
Sallies, drives the Enemy from th[eir]
Works, beats them out of their Trench[es,]
kills several of their Officers, and fin[ds]
Letters about them that afforded [us]
Intelligence, and particularly instruct[ed]
us about the Surrender of *Culmore*; [but]
upon what Conditions, and for how mu[ch]
Money, we could not understand.

Sallies were ordered after this Ma[n]-
ner: Captain *Noble*, and sometimes oth[er]
Officers, when they saw the Ener[my]
make an Approach, would run out wi[th]
abo[ut]

about ten or twelve Men at their Heels, and skirmish'd a while with them: When the Besieged saw them engaged, and in any Danger, they issued out in greater Numbers to their Relief, and always came off with great Execution on the Enemy, and with very little Loss to themselves.

In all these Sallies we lost none of any Note, but Lieutenant *Douglas*, and Captain *Cunningham*, " whom the Enemy " took Prisoner, and after Quarter given, " basely murdered." They did not want being reproached with so signal an Instance of their Cruelty and Inhumanity; neither did they want Impudence to deny it, by the Addition of many bloody Oaths and Protestations: But it was too evident by the Testimony of their own Officers and Soldiers, that were afterwards our Prisoners. " But this Sort of Pro-
" ceeding was very usual with them,
" and agreeable to an Account we had
" of their Obligation by Oath and Re-
" solutions, not to keep Faith with us,
" and to break whatever Articles were
given

" given us: A Prisoner with us was
" troubled in his Conscience, that he had
" engaged himself in so wicked a De-
" sign, and discovered it to us."

We were convinced of the Truth of it by some Examples they gave us after this: " When they hung out a *white* " *Flag* to invite us to a Treaty, Mr. " *Walker* ventured out to come within " hearing of my Lord *Lowth* and Colo- " nel *O'Neale*, and in his Passage had " an Hundred Shot fired at him;" he got the Shelter of a House, and upbraided them with this perfidious Dealing, and bid them order their Men to be quiet, or he would order all the Guns on the Walls to fire at them, they denied they were concerned, or knew any thing of it: And this was all the Satisfaction to be expected from Persons of such a Principle. At another Time the Enemy desired one *White* might have Leave to come to them, the Besieged sent him in a little Boat, with two Men, upon Parole, which they broke very dishonourably, keeping both the Men and Boat with them.

them. The Loss of the Boat was considerable to us; for the Gentlemen that left us, used all our Boats, and left them to the Sea and Wind; and this was the only Boat they had left.

The Enemy remove their main Body from *St. Johnstown*, and pitch their Tents upon *Bely-ugry-hill*, about two Miles distant from *Derry*, S. S. W. They place Guards on all Sides of the Town, so that the Besieged found it impossible to receive or convey any Intelligence, and great Difficulty to come to the Wells for Water, which they often fought for, and cost some of them their Blood. One Gentleman had a Bottle broke at his Mouth by a Shot; yet the Water of the Town was so muddy and troubled with our continual Firing, that we were forced to run those Hazards.

June 4. The Besiegers make an Attack at the *Windmill-works*, with a Body of Foot and Horse; the Horse they divided into three Squadrons, and assaulted us at the River-side, it being Low-Water; the

Foot attack the rest of our Line. The Front of the Horse was composed of Gentlemen that had bound themselves by an Oath, that they would mount our Line; they were commanded by Capt. *Butler*, second Son to my Lord *Montgarret*. Our Men place themselves within our Line in three Ranks, so advantageously that one Rank was always ready to march up and relieve the other, and discharge successively upon the Enemy, which (tho' 'tis strange how they could think otherwise) was great Surprize and Astonishment to them; for they, it seems, expected we should make but one single Volley, and then they could fall in upon us. Their Foot had Faggots laid before them for a Defence against our Shot; they and the Horse began with a loud Huzza, which was seconded from all Parts of their Camp with most dreadful Shrieks and Howlings of a numerous Rabble that attended the Enemy. The Faggot-men are not able to stand before our Shot, but are forced to quit their *new* Defence and run for it: Captain *Butler* tops our Work, which was but a dry Bank of
seven

seven Feet high at the Water-side, and thirty of his *sworn* Party of Horse follow him. Our Men wondered to find they had spent so many Shot, and that none of them fell: But Captain *Crooke* observed they had Armour on, and then commanded to fire at their Horses, which turned to so good Account, that but three of these bold Men with much Difficulty made their Escape. We wondered the Foot did not (according to Custom) run faster, till we took Notice, that in their Retreat they took the Dead on their Backs, and so preserved their own Bodies from the Remainder of our Shot, which was more Service than they did when alive.

The Enemy in this Action lost 400 of their Fighting Men; most of their Officers were killed. Captain *Butler* was taken Prisoner, and several others. We lost on our Side six private Men, and one Captain *Maxwell*; two of the Men were killed by a Shot of a great Gun from the other Side of the Water, opposite to the *Windmill-works*.

This Night the Enemy from *Strong Orchard* play their Bombs, which were 273 lb. Weight a-piece, and contained several Pounds of Powder in the Shell; they ploughed up our Streets, and broke down our Houses, so that there was no passing the Streets, nor staying within Doors, but all flock to the Walls and the remotest Parts of the Town, where we continued very safe, while many of our Sick were killed, being not able to leave their Houses: They plied the Besieged so close with great Guns in the Day-Time, and Bombs in the Night, and sometimes in the Day, that they could not enjoy their Rest, but were hurried from Place to Place, and tired into Faintness and Diseases, which destroyed many of the Garrison, which was reduced to 6185 Men the 15th of this Month. These Bombs were some Advantage to us, on one Account; for being under great Want of Fuel, they supplied us plentifully from the Houses they threw down, and the Timber they broke for us.

July

July 7. Three Ships came up to *Killmore-fort*, and fired at the Castle, and attempted coming up the River; but one of them unfortunately run aground, and lay some Time at the Mercy of the Enemy's Shot, and so much on her Side, she could not make any Return; but at length with some Pleasure we saw her get off; and, as we believed, without much Loss or Damage.

June 15. We discovered a Fleet of thirty Sail of Ships in the Lough, which we believed came from *England* for our Relief; but we could not propose any Method to get Intelligence from them, and we did fear it was impossible they could get to us; and the Enemy now begin to watch us more narrowly. They raise Batteries opposite to the Ships, and line both Sides of the River with great Numbers of Firelocks. They draw down their Guns to *Charles-Fort*, a Place of some Strength upon the narrow Part of of the River, where the Ships were to pass; here they contrived to place a Boom of Timber, joined by Iron Chains, and
fortified

fortified by a Cable of twelve Inches thic[k] twisted round it, they made this Boo[m] first of Oak, but that could not floa[t] and was soon broke by the Force of th[e] Water: Then they made one of Fir[r] beams, which answered their Purpose bet[-]ter; it was fasten'd at one End throug[h] the Arch of a Bridge, at the other by [a] Piece of Timber forced into the Groun[d] and fortified with a Piece of Stone-work[.] This Account, as we had it from th[e] Prisoners, did much trouble us, and scarc[e] left us any Hopes: We made severa[l] Signs to the Ships from the Steeple, an[d] they to us from their Ships, but wit[h] very little Information to either. " A[t] " last a Messenger got to us, one *Roch*[,] " from Major-General *Kirk*, who got t[o] " the Water-side over-against us, an[d] " then swam cross the River; he gav[e] " us an Account of the Ships, Men, " Provision and Arms in them for ou[r] " Relief; the great Concern of the Ma-
" jor-General for us, and his Care an[d] " Desire to get with his Ships up to the " Town" He sent another Messenger along with this, one *Crumy* a *Scotchman*,

to

to give us this Account, and to know the Condition of our Garrison; but he was taken Prisoner: There was soon an Understanding between him and the Enemy; he is instructed to frame a Message much differing from the other, they hang out a white Flag, inviting us to a Parley; they tell us we are under great Mistakes about the Major-General, and our Expectation of Relief from *England*; and that we might have Leave to inform ourselves further from the Messenger they had taken, either in private or publick: We sent some to that Purpose; but they soon discovered the Cheat, and returned to us with other particular Accounts of his Treachery.

We received further Intelligence in *July* by a little Boy, that, with great Ingenuity, made two Dispatches to us from the Major-General at *Inch*. One Letter he brought tied in his Garter; another, at his second coming, within a Cloth Button. We sent our first Answer made up within a Piece of a Bladder, in the Shape of a Suppositor, and the same was applied to the Boy; our second Answer he carried within

within the Folding of his Breeches, and falling among the Enemy, for Fear of a Discovery, he swallowed the Letter; and after some short Confinement and Endeavour to extort something from him, he made his Escape again to the Major-General.

Major-General *KIRK*'s Letter to Mr. *WALKER*.

SIR,

I Have received your's by the way of Inch: I writ to you Sunday last, that I would endeavour all means imaginable for your Relief, and find it impossible by the River, which made me send a Party to Inch, where I am going myself to try if I can beat off their Camp, or divert them, so that they shall not press you. I have sent Officers, Ammunition, Arms, great Guns, &c. to Iniskillin, who have 3000 Foot and 1500 Horse, and a Regiment of Dragoons, that has promised to come to their Relief, and at the same Time I will attack the Enemy by Inch; I expect

6000

6000 *Men from* England *every Minute, they having been shipped these eight Days; I have Stores and Victuals for you, and am resolved to relieve you.* England *and* Scotland *are in a good Posture, and all Things very well settled, be good Husbands of your Victuals, and by God's Help we shall overcome these barbarous People: Let me hear from you as often as you can, and the Messenger shall have what Reward he will. I have several of the Enemy has deserted to me, who all assure me they cannot stay long: I hear from* Inniskillin, *the Duke of* Berwick *is beaten; I pray God it be true; for then nothing can hinder them joining you or me. Sir,*

Your faithful Servant,

J. KIRKE.

To Mr. G. WALKER.

But to return to our Story: The Besieged send many a longing Look towards the Ships, their Allowance being very small, as you may see by the Account of Allowances out of the Store: They build a Boat of eight Oars a Side, and man it well, with Intent to make to the Fleet, and give the Major General an Account of the sad Condition we were in; they set out with the best of our Wishes and Prayers, but were forced to return, it being impossible they could endure the Showers of Shot that were poured in upon them from each Side the River.

June 18. Capt. *Noble* went up the River, and took twenty Men along with him, with a Design to rob the Fishhouse, but was prevented by Alarm from the Enemy's Boats; however he engaged them, killed a Lieutenant, one Ensign, and five private Men, took fourteen Prisoners and both their Boats. The Boats we offered to return, and to give the best Prisoner we had, for Leave to send a Messenger on an Errand to the Ships; but we could not prevail: Though we agreed for 500*l.* for Lieutenant-Colonel *Talbot*, (commonly called *Wicked Will*) we proffered him, and to remit the Money on the same Score, but we could not obtain this Favour upon any Terms: Soon after the Lieutenant-Colonel died of his Wounds, and we lost the Benefit of our Bargain; though we took all imaginable Care to keep him alive, permitted him his Surgeon and Diet from the Enemy, at Times agreed on; Favours that we allowed all the Prisoners, when we were starving ourselves; which we did not put any great Value on, but that the Enemy so ill deserved them. At this Time Governor *Baker* is very dangerously ill, and Colonel *Michelburn* is chosen and appointed to assist Gov. *Walker*, that when one commanded in Sallies the other might take Care of the Town; and if one should fall, the Town might not be left without a Government, and to the Hazard of new Elections.

June 24. or thereabouts, *Conrad de Rosen*, Marshal-General of the *Irish* Forces, is received into the Enemy's Camp, and finding how little the Enemy had prevailed

against

against us, expressed himself with great Fury against us, and swore *by the Belly of God*, He would demolish our Town and bury us in its Ashes, putting all to the Sword, without Consideration of Age or Sex, and would study the most exquisite Torments to lengthen the Misery and Pain of all he found obstinate, or active in opposing his Commands and Pleasure: But these Threatenings, as well as his Promises, in which he was very eloquent and obliging, had very little Power with us; " God having, under all our Difficulties, " established us with a Spirit and Resolu- " tion above all Fear or Temptation to any " mean Compliances, we having devoted " our Lives to the Defence of our City, " our Religion, and the Interest of King " *William* and Queen *Mary*."

For Fear any one should contrive surrendering the Town, or move it to the Garrison, " the Governor made an Order, " That no such Thing should be mention- " ed upon Pain of Death."

Every

Every Day some or other deserted the Garrison, so that the Enemy received constant Intelligence of our Proceedings. This gave some Trouble, and made us remove our Ammunition very often, and contrive many other Amusements. "Our "*Iron Ball* is now all spent, and instead "of them we make *Balls* of *Brick* cast "over with *Lead*, to the Weight and Size "of our *Iron Ball*." The Gunners did not pretend to be great Artists, yet they were very industrious, and scarce spent a Shot without doing some remarkable Execution.

The *Marshal de Rosen* orders three Mortar-Pieces and several Pieces of Ordnance against the *Windmill* Side of the Town, as also two Culverins opposite to *Butchers-gate*: He runs a Line out of *Bog-street* up within ten Perches of the Half-bastion of that Gate, in order to prepare Matters for laying and springing a Mine; he made Approaches to our Line, designing to hinder the Relief of our Out-guards, and to give us Trouble in fetching Water from *Colum-kills Well*, he defends his Line
with

with a strong Guard, in Hopes to seize our Out-works if we should chance to be negligent in our Posts, and neglect keeping good Guards. By the Contrivance of our Governor and Col. *Michelburn*, and the Directions and Care of Capt. *Shomberg*, or rather being instructed by the Working, Motions, and Example of the Enemy, as well as we could observe them, we countermine the Enemy before the *Butchersgate*, the Governor contrives a Blind to preserve our Work from the Enemy's Battery. The Enemy fired continually from their Trenches, and we make them due Returns with sufficient Damage to them. For, few Days passed but some of the choice and most forward of their Men fell by our Arms and Firing.

June 30. At ten of the Clock at Night my Lord *Clancarty* at the Head of a Regiment, and with some Detachments, possesses himself of our Line, and enters some Mines in a low Cellar under the Half-bastion. Captain *Noble*, Captain *Dunbar*, and several other Gentlemen sally by Order at the *Bishops-gate*, and creep
along

along the Wall till they came very near the Enemy's Guards; our Men receive their firing quietly till they got to a right Diſtance, and then thundered upon them. Our Caſe-ſhot from the Baſtion and ſmall Shot off the Walls ſecond the Salliers Firing ſo effectually, that his Lordſhip was forced to quit his Poſt and haſten to the main Body of the Enemy, and to leave his Miners and an Hundred of his beſt Men dead upon the Place; beſides, ſeveral Officers and Soldiers were wounded, and died of their Wounds ſome Days after this Action, as we were informed. We were often told, that ſome great Thing was to be performed by this Lord; and they had a *Prophecy* among them, *That a* Clancarty *ſhould knock at the Gates of* Derry; the Credulity and Superſtition of his Country, with the Vanity of ſo brave an Attempt, and ſome good Liquor, eaſily warmed him to this bold Undertaking, " but we ſee how little " Value is to be put on *Iriſh* Prophecies, " or Courage ſo ſupported."

June 30. GOVERNOR *Baker* dies; his Death was a ſenſible Loſs to us, and generally

rally lamented, being a valiant Person; in all his Actions among us, he shewed the greatest Honour, Courage and Conduct, and would it suit a Design of a Journal, we might fill a great Share of this Account with his Character.

And indeed there were so many great Things done by all our Officers and Men, and so often, that 'tis impossible to account them all; but certainly never People in the World behaved themselves better; and they cannot want mentioning upon other Occasion, where it may be more to their Advantage than to fill this Paper with their Story.

About this Time Lieutenant-General *Hamilton* offers Conditions to the Garrison, and they seem to hearken to them, till they had used that Opportunity to search for Provision to support the great Necessity of the Garrison, " which was now brought
" to that Extremity that they were forced
" to feed upon Horse-flesh, Dogs, Cats,
" Rats and Mice, Greaves of a Year old,
" Tallow, and Starch, of which they
" had

" had good Quantities, as also salted and
" dried Hides, &c. yet they unanimously
" resolved to eat the *Irish*, and then one
" another, rather than surrender to any
" but their own King *William* and Queen
" *Mary*." Our Answer to the Lieutenant-General was, *That we much wondered he should expect we could place any Confidence in him, that had so unworthily broke Faith with our King. That he was once generously trusted, though an Enemy, yet betrayed his Trust, and we could not believe that he had learned more Sincerity in an* Irish *Camp*.

GEN. *Rosen* sends us a Letter to this Effect, *That if we did not deliver the Town to him by Six of the Clock in the Afternoon on the first Day of* July, *according to Lieutenant-General* Hamilton's *Proposals, he would dispatch his Orders as far as* Balishanny, Charlimont, Belfast, *and the Barony of* Inishowen, *and rob all protected, as well as unprotected* Protestants, *that were either related to us, or of our Faction; and that they should be driven under the Walls of* Derry, *where they should perish, if not relieved by the Besieged.* He threatened, *to burn and lay waste*

waste all our Country, if there should appear the least Probability of any Troops coming for our Relief: Yet, if the Garrison would become Loyalists (as they termed it) and surrender the Town on any tolerable Conditions, he would protect them from all Injuries, and give them his Favour. But the Besieged receive all these Proposals with Contempt and some Indignation, which did produce some Heat and Disorder in the Marshal.

Among the Bombs thrown into Town, there was one dead Shell, in which was a Letter declaring to the Soldiers the Proposals made by the Lieutenant-General, for they imagined them Strangers to their Condescensions, and that their Officers would not communicate such Things to them. Copies also of these Proposals were conveyed into Town by Villains, who dispersed them about the Town; but all to no Purpose; for they will not entertain the least Thought of surrendering; " and it " would cost a Man's Life to speak of it, " it was so much abhorred."

July

July 2. " THE Enemy drive the poor Proteſtants, according to their Threatening, under our Walls, protected and unprotected, Men, Women and Children, and under great Diſtreſſes." Our Men at firſt did not underſtand the Meaning of ſuch a Crowd, but fearing they might be Enemies, fired upon them; we were troubled when we found the Miſtake, but it ſupported us to a great Degree when we found that none of them were touched by our Shot, which by the Direction of Providence (as if every Bullet had its Commiſſion what to do) ſpared them, and found out and killed three of the Enemy, that were ſome of thoſe that drove the poor People into ſo great a Danger. There were ſome Thouſands of them, " and they did move great Compaſſion in us, but warmed us with new Rage and Fury againſt the Enemy; ſo that in Sight of their Camp we immediately erected a Gallows, and ſignified to them, we were reſolved to hang their Friends, that were our Priſoners, if they did not ſuffer theſe poor People to return to their own Houſes."

We send to the Enemy, that the Prisoners might have Priests to prepare them, after their own Methods, for Death; but none came. We upbraid them with Breach of Promises, and the Prisoners detect their Barbarity, declaring, *They could not blame us to put them to Death, seeing their People exercised such Severity and Cruelty upon our poor Friends, that were under their Protections.* They desired Leave from the Governor, to write to Lieutenant-General *Hamilton*; they had a much better Opinion of him than we could be persuaded into; yet we allow a Messenger to carry the following Letter to him from their Prisoners.

My Lord,

UPON the hard Dealing the protected (as well as other Protestants) have met withal in being sent under the Walls, you have so incensed the Governor and others of this Garrison, that we are all condemned by a Court-martial to die To-morrow, unless those poor People be withdrawn. We have made Application to Marshal-General de Rosen;

Rosen; *but having received no Answer, we make it our Request to you (as knowing you are a Person that does not delight in shedding innocent Blood) that you will represent our Condition to the Martial General. The Lives of twenty Prisoners lie at Stake, and therefore require your Diligence and Care. We are all willing to die (with our Swords in our Hands) for his Majesty; but to suffer like Malefactors is hard, nor can we lay our Blood to the Charge of the Garrison, the Governor and the rest having used and treated us with all Civility imaginable. We remain*

Your most dutiful and dying Friends,

Netervill, Writ by another Hand, he himself having lost the Fingers of his Right Hand.

E. Butler, G. Aylmor,

—— *M'Donnel,*

—— *Darcy,* &c.

In the Name of all the rest.

To L. G. HAMILTON.

THE

The Lieutenant-General, to shew his great Concern for his Friends, returns this Answer to our Prisoners Letter.

Gentlemen,

IN Answer to yours: What those poor People are like to suffer, they may thank themselves for, being their own Fault; which they may prevent by accepting the Conditions which have been offer'd them; and if you suffer in this it cannot be help'd, but shall be revenged on many Thousands of those People (as well innocent as others) within or without that City.

Yours,

R. HAMILTON.

But however, the Sight of our Gallows, and the Importunity of some Friends of those that were to suffer upon them, prevailed upon the Lieutenant-General: So that *July* 4, the poor Protestants have Leave to repair to their several Habitations. We took down the Gallows, and ordered the Prisoners to their usual Apartments.

Our Garrison now confisted of 5709 Men, and to leffen our Number yet more, we crowded 500 of our ufelefs People among the Proteftants under the Walls, who paffed undifcovered with them, though the Enemy fufpected the Defign; and to diftinguifh them, they pretended of finding them out by the Smell. We alfo got into our Garrison fome effectual Men out of their Number: They were in a moft miferable Condition, " yet dreaded no-
" thing more than our Pity of them, and
" Willingnefs to receive them; begging
" of us on their Knees, not to take them
" into the Town, but chofe rather to pe-
" rifh under our Walls, than to hazard us
" within them."

THE Governor has feveral Intimations given him by a Friend in the Enemy's Camp, That he fhould look to himfelf, that fome Mifchief was intended him. Soon after this he underftood fome Jealoufy was entertained among the Soldiers, That he had great Quantity of Provifions hid in his Houfe. Some of the Garrifon improved this to that Degree, that there was

great

great Danger of a Mutiny among the Men, and that he then began to remember the Caution was given; but by Instructions to a Soldier, that was to pretend he himself had the same Suspicion, it was contrived that the House was privately searched, and their Curiosity being satisfied, they return to the good Opinion of their Governor.

He observed likewise, that the Enemy had endeavoured to insinuate to the Garrison, That he was to betray the Town to King *James*, and was to be highly prefered for the Service. This put them in Mind of a Message that one Mr. *Cole* brought to Mr *Walker* in the Beginning of *May* last, and however it was then suppressed, the Story is now revived, and the Governor in some Danger ——— Mr. *Cole* being taken by the Enemy, and continuing their Prisoner for some Time, is at last admitted to some Discourse with the Lieutenant-General, who enquired particularly, What Sort of Person Mr. *Walker* was; who he was most intimate with? Mr. *Cole* (among several of Mr. *Walker's* Friends) at last names himself, hoping by this Means to be employed on a Message to him, and to obtain his Liberty. The Lieutenant-General asked, *Whether he would do Service for K James, and carry some Proposals he had Orders to make to Mr.* Walker? He told him he would; and upon this immediately he has a Pass given him, and is dispatched upon a Message to Mr. *Walker.* Mr. *Cole* being got safe into the Town, was received with great Joy, and so well pleased with his Liberty that he forgot his Business, only casually mentions it to some of the Garrison, with other Discourse. Mr *Walker* (after this) meeting several of them, they saluted him by some great Names and Titles.

Mr. *Walker* easily saw the Danger of this, and finding it was occasioned by Discourses of Mr. *Cole's,* he ordered him immediately to be confined, and being examined, he unriddles the Mystery, and gave all People Satisfaction, so that they remained in no more Doubt of their Governor.

But under these, and many other such-like Difficulties, the Governor (not without some Trouble and Industry) re-assumed his Credit with the Garrison, which God was pleased to preserve to him, in Spite of all the Inventions and Designs to the contrary.

From our Works we could talk with the Enemy; several of our Men gave Account of Discourses with the *Irish*, *That they expressed great Prejudice and Hatred of the* French, *cursing those damn'd Fellows that walked in Trunks,* meaning their Jack-boots, " that had all Preferments in the Ar-
" my that fell, and took the Bread out of
" their Mouths, and they believed would have
" all the Kingdom to themselves at last."

	Men.
July 8. The Garrison now is reduced to	5520
13. The Garrison reduced to	5313
17. The Garrison reduced to	5114
22. The Garrison reduced to	4973
25. The Garrison reduced to	4892

This Day the Besieged made another Sally, which was performed after this Manner: The Day before we had a Council

cil of War, and all sworn to Secresy; the Result of which was, That the next Day at three in the Morning 200 Men should sally out of *Bishops-gate*, 200 Men at *Butchers-gate*, and 1100 should be ready within the Ravelin for a Reserve. Our Design was to bring in some of the Enemy's Cattle, they surprized the Enemy in their Trenches. One Regiment draws up against them in good Order, but had only three Matches lighted; we came upon them over-against *Butchers-gate*, and killed 300 of their Men, besides Officers. The Execution had been much greater, but many of our Men being much weakened with Hunger, were not able to pursue them, some falling with their own Blows. We returned without any Purchase of Cattle, but were advised to a more easy Experiment; having one Cow left, we ty'd her to a Stake and set Fire to her. We had Hopes given us, that by the Cry and Noise she would make, the Enemy's Cattle would be disturbed and come to her Relief; and they began to move and set up their Tails, so that we hoped to have gained our Point; but

but the Cow got loose, and turned to no Account, only the Danger of losing her.

July 27. The Garrison is reduced to 4456 Men, " and under the greatest Extremity
" for Want of Provision, which does ap-
" pear by this Account taken by a Gen-
" tleman in the Garrison, of the Price of
" our Food:

	s.	d.
" Horse-flesh *(per* ℔*)* sold for	1	8
" A Quarter of a Dog *(fattened by eating the Bodies of the slain* Irish*)*	5	6
" A Dog's Head	2	6
" A Cat	4	6
" A Rat	1	0
" A Mouse	0	6
" A small Flook taken in the River " not to be bought for Money, " or purchased under the Rate " of a Quantity of Meal.		
" A Pound of Greaves	1	0
" A Pound of Tallow	4	0
" A Pound of salted Hides	1	0
" A Quart of Horse-blood	1	0
" A Horse-pudding	0	6
" A Handful of Sea-wreck	0	2

" A Handful of Chickweed   0   1
" A Quart of Meal when found   1   0

We were under so great Necessity, that we had nothing left, unless we could prey upon one another: A certain fat Gentleman conceived himself in the greatest Danger, and fancying several of the Garrison looked on him with a greedy Eye, thought fit to hide himself for three Days. Our Drink was nothing but Water, which we paid very dear for, and could not get without great Danger; we mixed in it Ginger and Annifeeds, of which we had great Plenty; our Necessity of eating the Composition of Tallow and Starch, did not only nourish and support us, but was an infallible Cure of the Looseness; and recovered a great many that were strangely reduced by that Distemper, and preserved others from it *.

* Note, That in the Midst of this Extremity, the Spirit and Courage of the Men was so great, that they were often heard to discourse confidently, and with some Anger contend, Whether they should take their *Debentures* in *Ireland* or in *France*, when alas! they could not promise themselves twelve Hours Life.

" THE

"The Governor being with good Reason apprehensive, that these Discouragements might at length overcome that Resolution the Garrison had so long continued, considers of all imaginable Methods to support them, and finding in himself still that Confidence, That God would not (after so long and miraculous a Preservation) suffer them to be a Prey to their Enemies, preaches in the Cathedral, and encourages their Constancy, and endeavours to establish them in it, by reminding them of several Instances of Providence given them since they first came into that Place, and of what Consideration it was to the Protestant Religion at this Time; and that they need not doubt, but that God would at last deliver them from the Difficulties they were under."

July 30. About an Hour after Sermon, being in the Midst of our Extremity, we saw some Ships in the Lough make towards us, and we soon discovered they were the Ships Major-Gen. *Kirk* had sent us, according to his Promise, When we could hold

out no longer, "that he would be sure to
"relieve us, to the Hazard of himself,
"his Men, and his Ships."

THE *Mountjoy* of *Derry*, Capt. *Browning* Commander, the *Phœnix* of *Colrain*, Capt. *Douglas* Master, being both loaden with Provision, were convoyed by the *Dartmouth* Frigate. "The Enemy fired most
"desperately upon them from the Fort of
"*Culmore*, and both Sides the River; and
"they made sufficient Returns, and with
"the greatest Bravery. The *Mountjoy* made
"a little Stop at the Boom, occasioned by
"her Rebound after striking and breaking
"it, so that she was run a-ground: Upon
"this the Enemy set up the loudest Huzzas,
"and the most dreadful to the Besieged that
"ever we heard; fired all their Guns upon
"her, and were preparing their Boats to
"board her: Our Trouble is not to be ex-
"pressed at this dismal Prospect; but by
"great Providence firing a Broadside the
"Shock loosen'd her, so that she got clear
"and passed their Boom." Capt *Douglas* all this while was engaged, and the *Dartmouth*

mouth gave them very warm Entertainment. At length the Ships got to us, to the inexpressible Joy and Transport of our distressed Garrison; for we only reckoned upon two Days Life, and had only nine lean Horses left, and among us all one Pint of Meal to each Man; " Hunger and " the Fatigue of War had so prevailed " among us, that of 7500 Men regi- " mented, we had now alive but about " 4300, whereof at least one fourth Part " were rendered unserviceable."

This brave Undertaking, added to the great Success God had blessed us with in all our Attempts, so discouraged the Enemy, that on the last of *July*, they ran away in the Night-Time, robb'd and burnt all before them for several Miles, leaving nothing with the Country People but what they hid the Night before, in which their Care was so great, that Provision grew very plentiful after it.

In

IN the next Morning our Men, after Refreshment with a proper Share of our new Provisions, went out to see what was become of the Enemy, they saw them on their March, and pursued them a little too far, so that the Rear-guard of the Enemy's Horse turned upon them, and killed seven of our Men.

THEY encamped at *Strabane*, but hearing of the Defeat of their Forces under Lieutenant-General *M'Carty*, by the *Inniskillin* Men, they removed their Camp, and thought fit to make some Haste to get farther off; they broke into Pieces four of their great Guns, and threw twelve Cart-loads of Arms and Ammunition into the River.

" THUS after 105 Days being close be-
" sieged by near 20,000 Men constantly
" supplied from *Dublin*, God Almighty was
" pleased in our greatest Extremity to
" send Relief, to the Admiration and Joy
" of all good People, and to the great
" Disappointment of so powerful and in-
" veterate

"veterate an Enemy;" who were concerned in Point of Interest, as well as Reputation, to have rendered themselves Masters of that Town.

The Enemy lost between eight and nine Thousand Men before our Walls, and a Hundred of their best Officers, according to the best Computation we could make of both, by the Information of the Prisoners we took; most of these fell by the Sword, the rest of Fevers and Flux, and the *French* Pox, which was very remarkable on the Bodies of several of their dead Officers and Soldiers.

We are now under some Impatience, to see Major-General *Kirk*, under God, our Deliverer.

Aug. 1. The Governor orders C. *White*, C. *Dobbin*, C. *J. Hamilton*, Capt. *Jenny* and Mr. *Jo. Fox*, both Clergymen, to wait on the Major-General at *Inch*, to give him an Account of the raising the Siege, and to carry him our Thanks, and to desire

sire him to come and receive the Garrison. The next Day the Major-General sent to us Colonel *Steward* and Colonel *Richards* the Engineer, to congratulate our Deliverance. On *Sunday* the Major-General came into the Town, and was received by the Governor, and the whole Garrison, with the greatest Joy and Acclamations. " The Governor " presents him with the Keys, but he " would not receive them. The next " Day the Governor (with several of " his Officers) dined with the Major- " General at *Inch*; he complimented " the Major-General with his Regiment, " That after doing the King all the " Service in his Power, he might re- " turn to his own Profession: But the " Major-General desired him to dispose " of it as he pleased, and accordingly " he gave it to Captain *White*, as a " Mark of his Respect, and the Gentle- " man's known Merit."

UPON this we call a Council at *Derry*; the Governor is prevailed on to go

to

to the King, and to carry an Addreſs from the Garriſon. The Garriſon is now formed, and of eight Regiments made into ſix. "After Aſſurance from the Ma-
"jor-General, of his Care and Favour to
"his Men, and particularly to his own
"Regiment, he took Leave of them, and
"embarked for *England*."

To the Most Excellent Majesty of

WILLIAM and MARY,

King and Queen of *England, Scotland, France* and *Ireland*, Defenders of the Faith, &c.

The humble ADDRESS *of the Governors, Officers, and other Gentlemen, in the City and Garrison of* LONDON-DERRY.

WE the most dutiful and loyal Subscribers of this Address, (out of a deep Sense of our late miserable Estate and Condition) do hereby return our due Acknowledgments to Almighty God, and to your sacred Majesty, and, under you, to the indefatigable Care of Major-Gen. *Kirk*, for our unexpected Relief by Sea, in Spite of all the Opposition of our industrious, but bloody and implacable Enemies; which Relief was no less wonderfully, than seasonably, conveyed to us, and that, at the very Nick of Time, when we (who survived many Thousands that died here of Famine during the Siege) were juſt ready to [be] cut off, and periſh, by the Hands of barb[a]rous, cruel, and inhuman Wretches; wh[o] no ſooner ſaw us delivered, and that the[y] could not compaſs their wicked Deſigns [a]gainſt this your Majeſty's City, and o[ur] Lives, (for which they thirſted) immed[i]ately ſet all the Country round us on Fir[e,] after having plundered, robbed, and ſtri[p]ped all the Proteſtants therein, as well tho[ſe] Perſons they themſelves granted Protectio[n] to, as others: We do therefore moſt ſi[n]cerely rejoice with all our Souls, and ble[ſs] God for all his ſingular and repeated Me[r]cies and Deliverances, and do for ever ado[re] the Divine Providence for your Majeſty['s] rightful and peaceable Acceſſion to the Im[-]perial Crown of theſe Kingdoms (the pr[o]claiming of which was juſtly celebrated [in] theſe Parts with univerſal Joy); and w[e] do with all humble Submiſſion preſent [to] your ſacred Majeſty our unfeigned Loyalt[y,] the moſt valuable Tribute we can give, [or] your Majeſty receive from us. And ſinc[e] the ſame Providence has (thro' much Di[f]ficulty) made us ſo happy as to be you[r] Subjects, we come in the like Humilit[y] to lay ourselves intirely at your royal Feet, and do most heartily and resolvedly offer and engage our Lives and Fortunes to your Service. And further, we do most unanimously join in a firm and unchangeable Vow and Resolution of improving all Occasions of becoming serviceable to your Majesty, in what Station soever it shall please God and your Majesty to place us; and will expose ourselves to all Hazards and Extremities to serve your Majesty against the common Enemy. From all which Promises, Vows and Services, we and every of us promise (without any Exception or Reserve) not to recede unto our Lives End. In Testimony of all which, we have hereunto subscribed our Names at *London-derry*, this 29th Day of *July*, *Anno Dom.* 1689.

Signed,

GEORGE WALKER,

With other Gentlemen, Inhabitants, to the Number of One Hundred and Forty-four.

The Number of Bombs thrown into the City of London-Derry, since the Beginning of the Siege.

	Big	Small.
April 24.		3
25.		3
27.		18
From April the 27th to the 4th of May, at several Times		6
June 2.	3	1
3.	28	
4.	37	
5.	22	
6.	30	
7.	6	
8.	36	
11.		28
13.	26	
21.		21
24.	6	
27.	13	
28.	22	
29.	10	
July 2.		22
3.		28
4.	14	
	253	130

	Big	Small
Brought over	253	130
July 5.	3	6
6.	5	
7.		18
8, & 10.		24
11.		4
14.		18
15.		24
16.		16
17.		14
18.		12
19.		22
21, 28.		28
	261	316

'Till *July* 22.   Total   577

July 22.   42 Cannon Balls thrown into the City, about 20 Pound Weight a-piece, before nine o'Clock in the Morning.

Six more the same Evening.

July 23.   20 more before Dinner.

Memorandum. That one of the great Bombs being brought to the Scale did weigh 272 Pound, after 17 Pound of Powder was emptied out of it. And that one of the smallest Bombs being emptied, did weigh 34 Pounds.

Just published, by L. Davis *and* C. Reymers, *against* Gray's-Inn, Holborn,

I. THE Second Volume of *An Estimate of the Manners and Principles of the Times.*

II. The Seventh Edition of the First Volume of this Work.

III. Essays on the *Characteristics* of the *Earl of* Shaftsbury.

IV. The *Use and Abuse of Externals in Religion.* A Sermon preached at the Consecration of St. *James's* Church in *Whitehaven.*

V. On *the Pursuit of False Pleasure, and the Mischiefs of immoderate Gaming.* A Sermon preached at the Abbey-Church at *Bath*, for promoting the Charity and Subscription towards the General Hospital in that City, *April* 22, 1750.

VI. Liberty, A Poem.

By the Rev. Dr. Brown.

CPSIA information can be obtained
at www.ICGtesting.com
Printed in the USA
BVHW08s0958051018
529390BV00013B/314/P